Trust & Truth

Set In Soul

This Journal Belongs To

_____

Dedicated To The Hearts Looking For A Place To Call Home

Table Of Contents

How To Use This Journal

Your lack of trust didn't just happen overnight. You didn't just start questioning anything and/or everything yesterday.

Your lack of trust could stem from:

- a combination of dishonest acts that you may have witnessed or experienced and just can't seem to forget
- a combination of false promises that were never fulfilled
- acts from people you thought you knew doing something you would never have envisioned them doing
- a fear that is learned from parents, grandparents, peers, society, and outside forces that scare you out of believing in something better
- decisions you have made that you regret

Wherever your lack of trust stems from, you are here to heal and conquer it. What you might think is protecting you may be the very thing hurting you. Knowing this is why you are here. Now is the time to conquer your trust issues, not only to get to the bottom of it, but also to defeat the attitude and actions that keep you away from future opportunities that can propel you toward greatness. Sometimes your trust issues hurt you because you believe if you keep yourself guarded, that guard will protect you. The truth is you have been trusting in the wrong things and in the wrong people. The Bible states, "It is better to take refuge in the LORD than to trust in man." – Psalms 118:8. When there is an understanding that EVERYONE has the capability to hurt and disappoint you, you learn to align your expectations with God and trust in God to deliver and bring forth into your life what is needed for the advancement of his purpose and the fulfillment of your prayers. As many prayers are answered through the use of people, it is time to tackle these trust issues so that you can experience the blessings that God has for you. When you start healing, you will realize your issue is never with person who hurt you, lied to you, or did not deliver on their promise. The issue is with where you placed your trust and the comprehension of what is taking place.

It is recommended that you fill out the daily prompt questions every morning so that you may notice your growth over time and begin thinking in a positive way. There are several areas in this journal for you to simply write down any thoughts that come to mind. The motivational quotes sprinkled throughout this journal are there to guide you through your journey. It is time to say goodbye to every trust issue holding you back and grow stronger with the confidence of new beliefs.

Section One:

Matters Between Me
And My Heart

I Don't Trust (Write Who And/Or What You Don't Trust):

I Don't Trust This Person/Situation Because:

I Feel Like A Fool For Believing:

I Feel Like Everytime I Believed In _____

I Always Got _____.

As Soon As There Are Any Signs Of Dishonesty I:

The Reasons Why I Don't Trust People:

When It Comes To Family, I Don't:

What Triggers My Disbelief In Someone?

It Is Hard For Me To Believe:

I Am Scared That:

What Hurts Me?

Do I Trust Myself?

I Believe My Decision Making Skills Are:

What Keeps Happening To Me?

When I Open Myself Up To Trusting Someone I Feel:

I Tend To Have Flashbacks Of:

In Order For Me To Believe In Someone Now, I Must Always Be Proven:

I Have Experienced:

Even When I Don't Have Real Evidence To Mistrust Someone, I Continue To Be Wary Because:

I Do Not Accept:

I Have Never Been Accepted As:

It Impacts My Self Esteem When:

Others Can See My Lack Of Confidence Because:

I Am Very Guarded About:

I Am Very Guarded Because:

If I Was To Be Hurt Again, I Would:

I Am Tired Of:

I Have A Fear Of:

Being Vulnerable To Me Means:

I Become Defensive When:

Feelings That I No Longer Show:

Questions I Don't Like To Answer:

Questions I Don't Like To Ask:

Questions I Love To Ask:

When I Don't Believe The Answer To A Question That I Have Asked, I Would:

When I Didn't Believe In Something That I've Seen Or Heard, I Would:

An Early Childhood Experience That I Remember Where I Felt Disappointed:

I Learned That In Order For Me To Rely On Someone's Word Or Someone's Action, I Must:

I No Longer Past Judgement On:

In Order For Me To Have Confidence In Myself:

In Order For Me To Build Trust In A Good Relationship:

My Lack Of Trust Shows Up Towards Others When:

When Someone Does Not Trust Me, I Feel:

What Do I Need To Do To Rebuild Trust Towards Others Who Do Not Trust Me?

What Do I Need To Do To Build Trust Back Towards Myself?

My Trust Issues Have Caused Me To Believe:

The Lie In My Trust Issues:

I Can Start Being Honest With Myself About:

For Me To Forgive, I Require:

Replaying Past Experiences In My Mind Causes Me To:

I Just Can't Bring Myself To (Based On What You Responded To On The Last Question):

Because Of What Happened In The Past (Write What Happened):

It's Easy For Me To Think The Worst Case Scenarios Because:

I Have Allowed Hurt To:

I Have Allowed Betrayal To:

I View Loyalty As:

When I Feel Like Someone Is Being Dishonest With Me, I Tend To:

I Communicate My Lack Of Trust Towards Someone Or Something By:

In Order For Me To Rebuild Trust With Someone I Love, I:

Saying Sorry Is Not Enough For Me Because (If Applicable):

I Feel Like I Need:

I Am Determined To Reset My Mind And Heart To:

I Know That Even When Someone Is Being Dishonest, I Do Not Have To:

I Know I Will Not Stop Myself From Receiving Love Or Giving Love
Because:

To Those Who Genuinely Want To Know More About Me, I Will Start
Opening Myself Up By:

Matters Between Me And My Heart

I Currently Trust:

Section Two:

Releasing Control

I Am Not Able To Trust Anyone With:

A Situation I've Been Holding On To Where I Have Trusted Someone With Something Personal And They Have Disappointed Me (This Can Be A Family Member, Business Responsibility, Money...):

Did The Person Try To Rectify The Situation?

Since Then (The Above Situation), I Have:

It Would Be So Much Easier If I Can:

Releasing Control

I Rarely Ask For:

Why (To The Above Prompt)?

I Am Scared That:

I Have Worked So Hard To:

I Feel The Need To Have Control Over:

My Need For Control Comes From:

When I Sense That I Am Losing Control, I Start To Feel:

When I Am Quick To Say No, I Know I Am Also Saying No To:

Am I Good At Being A Team Player?

I Believe I Must Do Everything Myself Because:

Releasing Control

In The Past I Have Manipulated:

I Have Manipulated Situations Because:

When I Attempt To Fix Other People's Mistakes, I Feel:

I Am Not Only Hurting Within Myself, But I Am Also Hurting For:

Do I Feel Like The People That I Trust Are Sincere?

Can I Trust People That I Do Not Respect?

Do I Respect People That I Do Not Trust?

Do People That I Want To Trust With Something Or Someone Close To Me Or Even A Responsibility Share Something Valuable With Me?

Can I Learn To Trust Others While Developing Good Boundaries?

Can I Speak Up For Myself?

Releasing Control

I Express Disappointment By:

I Am Tired Of Trying To:

I Hold Everyone To This Standard (Write Your Standard):

I Now Believe Everyone Is:

Do I Believe I Am Just Like Everyone Else?

The Things That I Have Worked For That I Am Not Willing To Put In Anybody's Hands:

I Know That I Need:

Little By Little I Know I Can:

If What I Trusted Into Someone's Hands Actually Worked Out, I Would Feel:

I Know That Not Everyone:

With Time I Am Understanding:

Is It Better To Trust No One Or Is It Better To Take Chances?

I Want To Take A Chance At:

I Am Willing To Take A Chance At:

I Will Start Slowly By:

I Will Start Handing More Responsibility Over To Those Who Can Help Me By:

I Hold On To What I've Built/Love So Tightly Because:

What Others Don't Understand Is:

I Believe I Am Completely Responsible For:

I Try To Control My Emotions By:

I Find Myself Micromanaging:

Not Knowing How Something Will Go Makes Me Feel:

I Look Forward To These Things Working Out:

Regardless Of It All, I Will Always Trust My Spirit Because:

I Know One Person's Mistake Is Not Everyone's So I:

Releasing Control

Even Though I Know The Responsibilities I Place In Someone's Hand Will Never Be Handled In The Exact Same Way I Would Handle It, I Believe:

I Am Learning To Build Trust With:

Trust & Truth

Date: _____   Mood: _____

Today I Am Taking A Leap Of Faith By:	I Believe:
What I Trust God To Do Today:	I Trust Myself To:
I Feel Free In Letting Go Of The Fear Of:	An Example Of Something That I Rely On Everyday That I Trust:
Something That Didn't Work Out For Me Yesterday That I Am Okay With:	It's Okay That I Cannot Control:
I Am Deciding That My Past Will No Longer Dictate:	Today's Pending Trust Transaction (Between You And Someone Else Where Both Of You Must Trust Each Other With Something Big And/Or Small):

Fill In At Night

The Result Of The Trust Transaction And How I Am Handling The Result: _____.

Trust & Truth

Date: Mood:

Today I Am Taking A Leap Of Faith By: I Believe:

What I Trust God To Do Today: I Trust Myself To:

I Feel Free In Letting Go Of The Fear   An Example Of Something That I Rely On
Of: Everyday That I Trust:

Something That Didn't Work Out For   It's Okay That I Cannot Control:
Me Yesterday That I Am Okay With:

I Am Deciding That My Past Will No   Today's Pending Trust Transaction
Longer Dictate: (Between You And Someone Else Where
                                          Both Of You Must Trust Each Other With
                                          Something Big And/Or Small):

Fill In At Night

The Result Of The Trust Transaction And How I Am Handling The Result: _____.

Trust & Truth

Date: Mood:

Today I Am Taking A Leap Of Faith By:	I Believe:
What I Trust God To Do Today:	I Trust Myself To:
I Feel Free In Letting Go Of The Fear Of:	An Example Of Something That I Rely On Everyday That I Trust:
Something That Didn't Work Out For Me Yesterday That I Am Okay With:	It's Okay That I Cannot Control:
I Am Deciding That My Past Will No Longer Dictate:	Today's Pending Trust Transaction (Between You And Someone Else Where Both Of You Must Trust Each Other With Something Big And/Or Small):

Fill In At Night

The Result Of The Trust Transaction And How I Am Handling The Result: _____.

I Use Forgiveness As A Tool To Move On.

I Tend To Test....

Trust & Truth

Date: _____   Mood: _____

Today I Am Taking A Leap Of Faith By:	I Believe:
What I Trust God To Do Today:	I Trust Myself To:
I Feel Free In Letting Go Of The Fear Of:	An Example Of Something That I Rely On Everyday That I Trust:
Something That Didn't Work Out For Me Yesterday That I Am Okay With:	It's Okay That I Cannot Control:
I Am Deciding That My Past Will No Longer Dictate:	Today's Pending Trust Transaction (Between You And Someone Else Where Both Of You Must Trust Each Other With Something Big And/Or Small):

Fill In At Night

The Result Of The Trust Transaction And How I Am Handling The Result: _____.

A Good

Relationship

Is One That

Is Built On

Honesty.

My Spirit
Never Fails
Me. That's
Why I
Listen To It.

Date: _____   Mood: _____

Today I Am Taking A Leap Of Faith By: | I Believe:

What I Trust God To Do Today: | I Trust Myself To:

I Feel Free In Letting Go Of The Fear Of: | An Example Of Something That I Rely On Everyday That I Trust:

Something That Didn't Work Out For Me Yesterday That I Am Okay With: | It's Okay That I Cannot Control:

I Am Deciding That My Past Will No Longer Dictate: | Today's Pending Trust Transaction (Between You And Someone Else Where Both Of You Must Trust Each Other With Something Big And/Or Small):

Fill In At Night

The Result Of The Trust Transaction And How I Am Handling The Result: _____.

Date: Mood:

Today I Am Taking A Leap Of Faith By:	I Believe:
What I Trust God To Do Today:	I Trust Myself To:
I Feel Free In Letting Go Of The Fear Of:	An Example Of Something That I Rely On Everyday That I Trust:
Something That Didn't Work Out For Me Yesterday That I Am Okay With:	It's Okay That I Cannot Control:
I Am Deciding That My Past Will No Longer Dictate:	Today's Pending Trust Transaction (Between You And Someone Else Where Both Of You Must Trust Each Other With Something Big And/Or Small):

Fill In At Night

The Result Of The Trust Transaction And How I Am Handling The Result: _____.

Date: _____   Mood: _____

Today I Am Taking A Leap Of Faith By:	I Believe:
What I Trust God To Do Today:	I Trust Myself To:
I Feel Free In Letting Go Of The Fear Of:	An Example Of Something That I Rely On Everyday That I Trust:
Something That Didn't Work Out For Me Yesterday That I Am Okay With:	It's Okay That I Cannot Control:
I Am Deciding That My Past Will No Longer Dictate:	Today's Pending Trust Transaction (Between You And Someone Else Where Both Of You Must Trust Each Other With Something Big And/Or Small):

Fill In At Night

The Result Of The Trust Transaction And How I Am Handling The Result: _____.

Trust & Truth

Date: _____ Mood: _____

Today I Am Taking A Leap Of Faith By:

I Believe:

What I Trust God To Do Today:

I Trust Myself To:

I Feel Free In Letting Go Of The Fear Of:

An Example Of Something That I Rely On Everyday That I Trust:

Something That Didn't Work Out For Me Yesterday That I Am Okay With:

It's Okay That I Cannot Control:

I Am Deciding That My Past Will No Longer Dictate:

Today's Pending Trust Transaction (Between You And Someone Else Where Both Of You Must Trust Each Other With Something Big And/Or Small):

Fill In At Night

The Result Of The Trust Transaction And How I Am Handling The Result: _____.

I Use To....

Trust & Truth

Date: Mood:

Today I Am Taking A Leap Of Faith By: I Believe:

What I Trust God To Do Today: I Trust Myself To:

I Feel Free In Letting Go Of The Fear   An Example Of Something That I Rely On
Of: Everyday That I Trust:

Something That Didn't Work Out For   It's Okay That I Cannot Control:
Me Yesterday That I Am Okay With:

I Am Deciding That My Past Will No   Today's Pending Trust Transaction
Longer Dictate: (Between You And Someone Else Where
                                          Both Of You Must Trust Each Other With
                                          Something Big And/Or Small):

Fill In At Night

The Result Of The Trust Transaction And How I Am Handling The Result: _____.

Trust & Truth

Date: _____   Mood: _____

Today I Am Taking A Leap Of Faith By: I Believe:

What I Trust God To Do Today: I Trust Myself To:

I Feel Free In Letting Go Of The Fear Of: An Example Of Something That I Rely On Everyday That I Trust:

Something That Didn't Work Out For Me Yesterday That I Am Okay With: It's Okay That I Cannot Control:

I Am Deciding That My Past Will No Longer Dictate: Today's Pending Trust Transaction (Between You And Someone Else Where Both Of You Must Trust Each Other With Something Big And/Or Small):

Fill In At Night

The Result Of The Trust Transaction And How I Am Handling The Result: _____.

50

Trust & Truth

Date: Mood:

Today I Am Taking A Leap Of Faith By: | I Believe:

What I Trust God To Do Today: | I Trust Myself To:

I Feel Free In Letting Go Of The Fear Of: | An Example Of Something That I Rely On Everyday That I Trust:

Something That Didn't Work Out For Me Yesterday That I Am Okay With: | It's Okay That I Cannot Control:

I Am Deciding That My Past Will No Longer Dictate: | Today's Pending Trust Transaction (Between You And Someone Else Where Both Of You Must Trust Each Other With Something Big And/Or Small):

Fill In At Night

The Result Of The Trust Transaction And How I Am Handling The Result: _____.

My Trust & Truth Notes

Trust & Truth

Date: Mood:

Today I Am Taking A Leap Of Faith By:	I Believe:
What I Trust God To Do Today:	I Trust Myself To:
I Feel Free In Letting Go Of The Fear Of:	An Example Of Something That I Rely On Everyday That I Trust:
Something That Didn't Work Out For Me Yesterday That I Am Okay With:	It's Okay That I Cannot Control:
I Am Deciding That My Past Will No Longer Dictate:	Today's Pending Trust Transaction (Between You And Someone Else Where Both Of You Must Trust Each Other With Something Big And/Or Small):

Fill In At Night

The Result Of The Trust Transaction And How I Am Handling The Result: _____.

Trust & Truth

Date: _____   Mood: _____

Today I Am Taking A Leap Of Faith By:	I Believe:
What I Trust God To Do Today:	I Trust Myself To:
I Feel Free In Letting Go Of The Fear Of:	An Example Of Something That I Rely On Everyday That I Trust:
Something That Didn't Work Out For Me Yesterday That I Am Okay With:	It's Okay That I Cannot Control:
I Am Deciding That My Past Will No Longer Dictate:	Today's Pending Trust Transaction (Between You And Someone Else Where Both Of You Must Trust Each Other With Something Big And/Or Small):

Fill In At Night

The Result Of The Trust Transaction And How I Am Handling The Result: _____.

Trust & Truth

Date: _____   Mood: _____

Today I Am Taking A Leap Of Faith By:	I Believe:
What I Trust God To Do Today:	I Trust Myself To:
I Feel Free In Letting Go Of The Fear Of:	An Example Of Something That I Rely On Everyday That I Trust:
Something That Didn't Work Out For Me Yesterday That I Am Okay With:	It's Okay That I Cannot Control:
I Am Deciding That My Past Will No Longer Dictate:	Today's Pending Trust Transaction (Between You And Someone Else Where Both Of You Must Trust Each Other With Something Big And/Or Small):

Fill In At Night

The Result Of The Trust Transaction And How I Am Handling The Result: _____.

My
Trust
Is In
God.

I Will Not Stop Believing That What I Ask For Will Appear. I Trust In God's Timing.

Trust & Truth

Date: _____   Mood: _____

Today I Am Taking A Leap Of Faith By:

I Believe:

What I Trust God To Do Today:

I Trust Myself To:

I Feel Free In Letting Go Of The Fear Of:

An Example Of Something That I Rely On Everyday That I Trust:

Something That Didn't Work Out For Me Yesterday That I Am Okay With:

It's Okay That I Cannot Control:

I Am Deciding That My Past Will No Longer Dictate:

Today's Pending Trust Transaction (Between You And Someone Else Where Both Of You Must Trust Each Other With Something Big And/Or Small):

Fill In At Night

The Result Of The Trust Transaction And How I Am Handling The Result: _____.

Trust & Truth

Date: Mood:

Today I Am Taking A Leap Of Faith By: | I Believe:

What I Trust God To Do Today: | I Trust Myself To:

I Feel Free In Letting Go Of The Fear Of: | An Example Of Something That I Rely On Everyday That I Trust:

Something That Didn't Work Out For Me Yesterday That I Am Okay With: | It's Okay That I Cannot Control:

I Am Deciding That My Past Will No Longer Dictate: | Today's Pending Trust Transaction (Between You And Someone Else Where Both Of You Must Trust Each Other With Something Big And/Or Small):

Fill In At Night

The Result Of The Trust Transaction And How I Am Handling The Result: _____.

Trust & Truth

Date: Mood:

Today I Am Taking A Leap Of Faith By: | I Believe:

What I Trust God To Do Today: | I Trust Myself To:

I Feel Free In Letting Go Of The Fear | An Example Of Something That I Rely On
Of: | Everyday That I Trust:

Something That Didn't Work Out For | It's Okay That I Cannot Control:
Me Yesterday That I Am Okay With: |

I Am Deciding That My Past Will No | Today's Pending Trust Transaction
Longer Dictate: | (Between You And Someone Else Where
                                       | Both Of You Must Trust Each Other With
                                       | Something Big And/Or Small):

Fill In At Night

The Result Of The Trust Transaction And How I Am Handling The Result: _____.

I Was Told....

What Actually

Happened....

My Trust & Truth Notes

Trust & Truth

Date: _____   Mood: _____

Today I Am Taking A Leap Of Faith By:

I Believe:

What I Trust God To Do Today:

I Trust Myself To:

I Feel Free In Letting Go Of The Fear Of:

An Example Of Something That I Rely On Everyday That I Trust:

Something That Didn't Work Out For Me Yesterday That I Am Okay With:

It's Okay That I Cannot Control:

I Am Deciding That My Past Will No Longer Dictate:

Today's Pending Trust Transaction (Between You And Someone Else Where Both Of You Must Trust Each Other With Something Big And/Or Small):

Fill In At Night

The Result Of The Trust Transaction And How I Am Handling The Result: _____.

Trust & Truth

Date: _____   Mood: _____

Today I Am Taking A Leap Of Faith By:	I Believe:
What I Trust God To Do Today:	I Trust Myself To:
I Feel Free In Letting Go Of The Fear Of:	An Example Of Something That I Rely On Everyday That I Trust:
Something That Didn't Work Out For Me Yesterday That I Am Okay With:	It's Okay That I Cannot Control:
I Am Deciding That My Past Will No Longer Dictate:	Today's Pending Trust Transaction (Between You And Someone Else Where Both Of You Must Trust Each Other With Something Big And/Or Small):

Fill In At Night

The Result Of The Trust Transaction And How I Am Handling The Result: _____.

Trust & Truth

Date: Mood:

Today I Am Taking A Leap Of Faith By: | I Believe:

What I Trust God To Do Today: | I Trust Myself To:

I Feel Free In Letting Go Of The Fear Of: | An Example Of Something That I Rely On Everyday That I Trust:

Something That Didn't Work Out For Me Yesterday That I Am Okay With: | It's Okay That I Cannot Control:

I Am Deciding That My Past Will No Longer Dictate: | Today's Pending Trust Transaction (Between You And Someone Else Where Both Of You Must Trust Each Other With Something Big And/Or Small):

Fill In At Night

The Result Of The Trust Transaction And How I Am Handling The Result: _____.

Trust & Truth

Date: _____   Mood: _____

Today I Am Taking A Leap Of Faith By:	I Believe:
What I Trust God To Do Today:	I Trust Myself To:
I Feel Free In Letting Go Of The Fear Of:	An Example Of Something That I Rely On Everyday That I Trust:
Something That Didn't Work Out For Me Yesterday That I Am Okay With:	It's Okay That I Cannot Control:
I Am Deciding That My Past Will No Longer Dictate:	Today's Pending Trust Transaction (Between You And Someone Else Where Both Of You Must Trust Each Other With Something Big And/Or Small):

Fill In At Night

The Result Of The Trust Transaction And How I Am Handling The Result: _____.

66

Trust & Truth

Date: _____   Mood: _____

Today I Am Taking A Leap Of Faith By:

I Believe:

What I Trust God To Do Today:

I Trust Myself To:

I Feel Free In Letting Go Of The Fear Of:

An Example Of Something That I Rely On Everyday That I Trust:

Something That Didn't Work Out For Me Yesterday That I Am Okay With:

It's Okay That I Cannot Control:

I Am Deciding That My Past Will No Longer Dictate:

Today's Pending Trust Transaction (Between You And Someone Else Where Both Of You Must Trust Each Other With Something Big And/Or Small):

Fill In At Night

The Result Of The Trust Transaction And How I Am Handling The Result: _____.

No One's
Opinion
Will
Determine
My Truth.

I've Learned To Forgive Acts Of Wrongdoing Without Punishing Myself.

I Believe

In

Love. I

Always

Will.

Date: Mood:

Today I Am Taking A Leap Of Faith By: | I Believe:

What I Trust God To Do Today: | I Trust Myself To:

I Feel Free In Letting Go Of The Fear Of: | An Example Of Something That I Rely On Everyday That I Trust:

Something That Didn't Work Out For Me Yesterday That I Am Okay With: | It's Okay That I Cannot Control:

I Am Deciding That My Past Will No Longer Dictate: | Today's Pending Trust Transaction (Between You And Someone Else Where Both Of You Must Trust Each Other With Something Big And/Or Small):

Fill In At Night

The Result Of The Trust Transaction And How I Am Handling The Result: _____.

Date: _____   Mood: _____

Today I Am Taking A Leap Of Faith By:	I Believe:
What I Trust God To Do Today:	I Trust Myself To:
I Feel Free In Letting Go Of The Fear Of:	An Example Of Something That I Rely On Everyday That I Trust:
Something That Didn't Work Out For Me Yesterday That I Am Okay With:	It's Okay That I Cannot Control:
I Am Deciding That My Past Will No Longer Dictate:	Today's Pending Trust Transaction (Between You And Someone Else Where Both Of You Must Trust Each Other With Something Big And/Or Small):

Fill In At Night

The Result Of The Trust Transaction And How I Am Handling The Result: _____.

Date: _____   Mood: _____

Today I Am Taking A Leap Of Faith By: I Believe:

What I Trust God To Do Today: I Trust Myself To:

I Feel Free In Letting Go Of The Fear   An Example Of Something That I Rely On
Of: Everyday That I Trust:

Something That Didn't Work Out For   It's Okay That I Cannot Control:
Me Yesterday That I Am Okay With:

I Am Deciding That My Past Will No   Today's Pending Trust Transaction
Longer Dictate: (Between You And Someone Else Where
                                         Both Of You Must Trust Each Other With
                                         Something Big And/Or Small):

Fill In At Night

The Result Of The Trust Transaction And How I Am Handling The Result: _____.

Trust & Truth

Date: _____   Mood: _____

Today I Am Taking A Leap Of Faith By:	I Believe:
What I Trust God To Do Today:	I Trust Myself To:
I Feel Free In Letting Go Of The Fear Of:	An Example Of Something That I Rely On Everyday That I Trust:
Something That Didn't Work Out For Me Yesterday That I Am Okay With:	It's Okay That I Cannot Control:
I Am Deciding That My Past Will No Longer Dictate:	Today's Pending Trust Transaction (Between You And Someone Else Where Both Of You Must Trust Each Other With Something Big And/Or Small):

Fill In At Night

The Result Of The Trust Transaction And How I Am Handling The Result: _____.

Five Ways I Handle Mixed Messages.....

1.

2.

3.

4.

5.

Trust & Truth

Date: Mood:

Today I Am Taking A Leap Of Faith By: I Believe:

What I Trust God To Do Today: I Trust Myself To:

I Feel Free In Letting Go Of The Fear Of: An Example Of Something That I Rely On Everyday That I Trust:

Something That Didn't Work Out For Me Yesterday That I Am Okay With: It's Okay That I Cannot Control:

I Am Deciding That My Past Will No Longer Dictate: Today's Pending Trust Transaction (Between You And Someone Else Where Both Of You Must Trust Each Other With Something Big And/Or Small):

Fill In At Night

The Result Of The Trust Transaction And How I Am Handling The Result: _____.

Trust & Truth

Date:

Mood:

Today I Am Taking A Leap Of Faith By:

I Believe:

What I Trust God To Do Today:

I Trust Myself To:

I Feel Free In Letting Go Of The Fear Of:

An Example Of Something That I Rely On Everyday That I Trust:

Something That Didn't Work Out For Me Yesterday That I Am Okay With:

It's Okay That I Cannot Control:

I Am Deciding That My Past Will No Longer Dictate:

Today's Pending Trust Transaction (Between You And Someone Else Where Both Of You Must Trust Each Other With Something Big And/Or Small):

Fill In At Night

The Result Of The Trust Transaction And How I Am Handling The Result: _____.

My Trust & Truth Notes

Trust & Truth

Date: Mood:

Today I Am Taking A Leap Of Faith By: | I Believe:

What I Trust God To Do Today: | I Trust Myself To:

I Feel Free In Letting Go Of The Fear | An Example Of Something That I Rely On
Of: | Everyday That I Trust:

Something That Didn't Work Out For | It's Okay That I Cannot Control:
Me Yesterday That I Am Okay With: |

I Am Deciding That My Past Will No | Today's Pending Trust Transaction
Longer Dictate: | (Between You And Someone Else Where
                                          | Both Of You Must Trust Each Other With
                                          | Something Big And/Or Small):

Fill In At Night

The Result Of The Trust Transaction And How I Am Handling The Result: _____.

Date: _____   Mood: _____

Today I Am Taking A Leap Of Faith By:	I Believe:
What I Trust God To Do Today:	I Trust Myself To:
I Feel Free In Letting Go Of The Fear Of:	An Example Of Something That I Rely On Everyday That I Trust:
Something That Didn't Work Out For Me Yesterday That I Am Okay With:	It's Okay That I Cannot Control:
I Am Deciding That My Past Will No Longer Dictate:	Today's Pending Trust Transaction (Between You And Someone Else Where Both Of You Must Trust Each Other With Something Big And/Or Small):

Fill In At Night

The Result Of The Trust Transaction And How I Am Handling The Result: _____.

Trust & Truth

Date: _____   Mood: _____

Today I Am Taking A Leap Of Faith By: I Believe:

What I Trust God To Do Today: I Trust Myself To:

I Feel Free In Letting Go Of The Fear Of: An Example Of Something That I Rely On Everyday That I Trust:

Something That Didn't Work Out For Me Yesterday That I Am Okay With: It's Okay That I Cannot Control:

I Am Deciding That My Past Will No Longer Dictate: Today's Pending Trust Transaction (Between You And Someone Else Where Both Of You Must Trust Each Other With Something Big And/Or Small):

Fill In At Night

The Result Of The Trust Transaction And How I Am Handling The Result: _____.

81

Date: Mood:

Today I Am Taking A Leap Of Faith By: | I Believe:

What I Trust God To Do Today: | I Trust Myself To:

I Feel Free In Letting Go Of The Fear Of: | An Example Of Something That I Rely On Everyday That I Trust:

Something That Didn't Work Out For Me Yesterday That I Am Okay With: | It's Okay That I Cannot Control:

I Am Deciding That My Past Will No Longer Dictate: | Today's Pending Trust Transaction (Between You And Someone Else Where Both Of You Must Trust Each Other With Something Big And/Or Small):

Fill In At Night

The Result Of The Trust Transaction And How I Am Handling The Result: _____.

I'm Opening Up Little By Little By....

I Don't Need Others To Love The Decisions I Am Making.

My
Spirit
Is My
Superpower.

Trust & Truth

Date: Mood:

Today I Am Taking A Leap Of Faith By:	I Believe:
What I Trust God To Do Today:	I Trust Myself To:
I Feel Free In Letting Go Of The Fear Of:	An Example Of Something That I Rely On Everyday That I Trust:
Something That Didn't Work Out For Me Yesterday That I Am Okay With:	It's Okay That I Cannot Control:
I Am Deciding That My Past Will No Longer Dictate:	Today's Pending Trust Transaction (Between You And Someone Else Where Both Of You Must Trust Each Other With Something Big And/Or Small):

Fill In At Night

The Result Of The Trust Transaction And How I Am Handling The Result: _____.

Trust & Truth

Date: Mood:

Today I Am Taking A Leap Of Faith By: | I Believe:

What I Trust God To Do Today: | I Trust Myself To:

I Feel Free In Letting Go Of The Fear Of: | An Example Of Something That I Rely On Everyday That I Trust:

Something That Didn't Work Out For Me Yesterday That I Am Okay With: | It's Okay That I Cannot Control:

I Am Deciding That My Past Will No Longer Dictate: | Today's Pending Trust Transaction (Between You And Someone Else Where Both Of You Must Trust Each Other With Something Big And/Or Small):

Fill In At Night

The Result Of The Trust Transaction And How I Am Handling The Result: _____.

The Predominant Feeling Behind The Lack Of Trust Is.....

I Let Go
Of Anger
So I Can
Live In
Peace.

Trust & Truth

Date: _____   Mood: _____

Today I Am Taking A Leap Of Faith By: | I Believe:

What I Trust God To Do Today: | I Trust Myself To:

I Feel Free In Letting Go Of The Fear Of: | An Example Of Something That I Rely On Everyday That I Trust:

Something That Didn't Work Out For Me Yesterday That I Am Okay With: | It's Okay That I Cannot Control:

I Am Deciding That My Past Will No Longer Dictate: | Today's Pending Trust Transaction (Between You And Someone Else Where Both Of You Must Trust Each Other With Something Big And/Or Small):

Fill In At Night

The Result Of The Trust Transaction And How I Am Handling The Result: _____.

Trust & Truth

Date: Mood:

Today I Am Taking A Leap Of Faith By: | I Believe:

What I Trust God To Do Today: | I Trust Myself To:

I Feel Free In Letting Go Of The Fear Of: | An Example Of Something That I Rely On Everyday That I Trust:

Something That Didn't Work Out For Me Yesterday That I Am Okay With: | It's Okay That I Cannot Control:

I Am Deciding That My Past Will No Longer Dictate: | Today's Pending Trust Transaction (Between You And Someone Else Where Both Of You Must Trust Each Other With Something Big And/Or Small):

Fill In At Night

The Result Of The Trust Transaction And How I Am Handling The Result: _____.

Trust & Truth

Date: _____   Mood: _____

Today I Am Taking A Leap Of Faith By: | I Believe:

What I Trust God To Do Today: | I Trust Myself To:

I Feel Free In Letting Go Of The Fear Of: | An Example Of Something That I Rely On Everyday That I Trust:

Something That Didn't Work Out For Me Yesterday That I Am Okay With: | It's Okay That I Cannot Control:

I Am Deciding That My Past Will No Longer Dictate: | Today's Pending Trust Transaction (Between You And Someone Else Where Both Of You Must Trust Each Other With Something Big And/Or Small):

Fill In At Night

The Result Of The Trust Transaction And How I Am Handling The Result: _____.

My Overthinking Causes Me To....

A Letter To Those I Would Like To Reestablish Trust With....

My Trust & Truth Notes

Date: _____   Mood: _____

Today I Am Taking A Leap Of Faith By:	I Believe:
What I Trust God To Do Today:	I Trust Myself To:
I Feel Free In Letting Go Of The Fear Of:	An Example Of Something That I Rely On Everyday That I Trust:
Something That Didn't Work Out For Me Yesterday That I Am Okay With:	It's Okay That I Cannot Control:
I Am Deciding That My Past Will No Longer Dictate:	Today's Pending Trust Transaction (Between You And Someone Else Where Both Of You Must Trust Each Other With Something Big And/Or Small):

Fill In At Night

The Result Of The Trust Transaction And How I Am Handling The Result: _____.

Being
Vulnerable
Doesn't Make
Me Weak.
Being
Vulnerable
Makes
Me Strong.

Trust & Truth

Date: _____   Mood: _____

Today I Am Taking A Leap Of Faith By:	I Believe:
What I Trust God To Do Today:	I Trust Myself To:
I Feel Free In Letting Go Of The Fear Of:	An Example Of Something That I Rely On Everyday That I Trust:
Something That Didn't Work Out For Me Yesterday That I Am Okay With:	It's Okay That I Cannot Control:
I Am Deciding That My Past Will No Longer Dictate:	Today's Pending Trust Transaction (Between You And Someone Else Where Both Of You Must Trust Each Other With Something Big And/Or Small):

Fill In At Night

The Result Of The Trust Transaction And How I Am Handling The Result: _____.

Trust & Truth

Date: _____   Mood: _____

Today I Am Taking A Leap Of Faith By:

I Believe:

What I Trust God To Do Today:

I Trust Myself To:

I Feel Free In Letting Go Of The Fear Of:

An Example Of Something That I Rely On Everyday That I Trust:

Something That Didn't Work Out For Me Yesterday That I Am Okay With:

It's Okay That I Cannot Control:

I Am Deciding That My Past Will No Longer Dictate:

Today's Pending Trust Transaction (Between You And Someone Else Where Both Of You Must Trust Each Other With Something Big And/Or Small):

Fill In At Night

The Result Of The Trust Transaction And How I Am Handling The Result: _____.

I Didn't
Lose Faith.
That's Why
I Can Still
Trust.

Even When
Others Can't
See What
I Believe,
I Know I
Have Made
Some Good
Decisions.

Trust & Truth

Date: Mood:

Today I Am Taking A Leap Of Faith By: | I Believe:

What I Trust God To Do Today: | I Trust Myself To:

I Feel Free In Letting Go Of The Fear Of: | An Example Of Something That I Rely On Everyday That I Trust:

Something That Didn't Work Out For Me Yesterday That I Am Okay With: | It's Okay That I Cannot Control:

I Am Deciding That My Past Will No Longer Dictate: | Today's Pending Trust Transaction (Between You And Someone Else Where Both Of You Must Trust Each Other With Something Big And/Or Small):

Fill In At Night

The Result Of The Trust Transaction And How I Am Handling The Result: _____.

Trust & Truth

Date: Mood:

Today I Am Taking A Leap Of Faith By:	I Believe:
What I Trust God To Do Today:	I Trust Myself To:
I Feel Free In Letting Go Of The Fear Of:	An Example Of Something That I Rely On Everyday That I Trust:
Something That Didn't Work Out For Me Yesterday That I Am Okay With:	It's Okay That I Cannot Control:
I Am Deciding That My Past Will No Longer Dictate:	Today's Pending Trust Transaction (Between You And Someone Else Where Both Of You Must Trust Each Other With Something Big And/Or Small):

Fill In At Night

The Result Of The Trust Transaction And How I Am Handling The Result: _____.

Trust & Truth

Date: _____   Mood: _____

Today I Am Taking A Leap Of Faith By: | **I Believe:**

What I Trust God To Do Today: | **I Trust Myself To:**

I Feel Free In Letting Go Of The Fear Of: | **An Example Of Something That I Rely On Everyday That I Trust:**

Something That Didn't Work Out For Me Yesterday That I Am Okay With: | **It's Okay That I Cannot Control:**

I Am Deciding That My Past Will No Longer Dictate: | **Today's Pending Trust Transaction (Between You And Someone Else Where Both Of You Must Trust Each Other With Something Big And/Or Small):**

Fill In At Night

The Result Of The Trust Transaction And How I Am Handling The Result: _____.

Trust & Truth

Date: _____   Mood: _____

Today I Am Taking A Leap Of Faith By:	I Believe:
What I Trust God To Do Today:	I Trust Myself To:
I Feel Free In Letting Go Of The Fear Of:	An Example Of Something That I Rely On Everyday That I Trust:
Something That Didn't Work Out For Me Yesterday That I Am Okay With:	It's Okay That I Cannot Control:
I Am Deciding That My Past Will No Longer Dictate:	Today's Pending Trust Transaction (Between You And Someone Else Where Both Of You Must Trust Each Other With Something Big And/Or Small):

Fill In At Night

The Result Of The Trust Transaction And How I Am Handling The Result: _____.

Date: _____   Mood: _____

Today I Am Taking A Leap Of Faith By:	I Believe:
What I Trust God To Do Today:	I Trust Myself To:
I Feel Free In Letting Go Of The Fear Of:	An Example Of Something That I Rely On Everyday That I Trust:
Something That Didn't Work Out For Me Yesterday That I Am Okay With:	It's Okay That I Cannot Control:
I Am Deciding That My Past Will No Longer Dictate:	Today's Pending Trust Transaction (Between You And Someone Else Where Both Of You Must Trust Each Other With Something Big And/Or Small):

Fill In At Night

The Result Of The Trust Transaction And How I Am Handling The Result: _____.

Trust & Truth

Date: _____   Mood: _____

Today I Am Taking A Leap Of Faith By:	I Believe:
What I Trust God To Do Today:	I Trust Myself To:
I Feel Free In Letting Go Of The Fear Of:	An Example Of Something That I Rely On Everyday That I Trust:
Something That Didn't Work Out For Me Yesterday That I Am Okay With:	It's Okay That I Cannot Control:
I Am Deciding That My Past Will No Longer Dictate:	Today's Pending Trust Transaction (Between You And Someone Else Where Both Of You Must Trust Each Other With Something Big And/Or Small):

Fill In At Night

The Result Of The Trust Transaction And How I Am Handling The Result: _____.

Trust & Truth

Date: _____   Mood: _____

Today I Am Taking A Leap Of Faith By: | I Believe:

What I Trust God To Do Today: | I Trust Myself To:

I Feel Free In Letting Go Of The Fear Of: | An Example Of Something That I Rely On Everyday That I Trust:

Something That Didn't Work Out For Me Yesterday That I Am Okay With: | It's Okay That I Cannot Control:

I Am Deciding That My Past Will No Longer Dictate: | Today's Pending Trust Transaction (Between You And Someone Else Where Both Of You Must Trust Each Other With Something Big And/Or Small):

Fill In At Night

The Result Of The Trust Transaction And How I Am Handling The Result: _____.

108

Five People That I Trust....

1.

2.

3.

4.

5.

My Trust & Truth Notes

Date: | Mood:

Today I Am Taking A Leap Of Faith By: | **I Believe:**

What I Trust God To Do Today: | **I Trust Myself To:**

I Feel Free In Letting Go Of The Fear Of: | **An Example Of Something That I Rely On Everyday That I Trust:**

Something That Didn't Work Out For Me Yesterday That I Am Okay With: | **It's Okay That I Cannot Control:**

I Am Deciding That My Past Will No Longer Dictate: | **Today's Pending Trust Transaction (Between You And Someone Else Where Both Of You Must Trust Each Other With Something Big And/Or Small):**

Fill In At Night

The Result Of The Trust Transaction And How I Am Handling The Result: _____.

Date: Mood:

Today I Am Taking A Leap Of Faith By:	I Believe:
What I Trust God To Do Today:	I Trust Myself To:
I Feel Free In Letting Go Of The Fear Of:	An Example Of Something That I Rely On Everyday That I Trust:
Something That Didn't Work Out For Me Yesterday That I Am Okay With:	It's Okay That I Cannot Control:
I Am Deciding That My Past Will No Longer Dictate:	Today's Pending Trust Transaction (Between You And Someone Else Where Both Of You Must Trust Each Other With Something Big And/Or Small):

Fill In At Night

The Result Of The Trust Transaction And How I Am Handling The Result: _____.

Trust & Truth

Date: _____   Mood: _____

Today I Am Taking A Leap Of Faith By:	I Believe:
What I Trust God To Do Today:	I Trust Myself To:
I Feel Free In Letting Go Of The Fear Of:	An Example Of Something That I Rely On Everyday That I Trust:
Something That Didn't Work Out For Me Yesterday That I Am Okay With:	It's Okay That I Cannot Control:
I Am Deciding That My Past Will No Longer Dictate:	Today's Pending Trust Transaction (Between You And Someone Else Where Both Of You Must Trust Each Other With Something Big And/Or Small):

Fill In At Night

The Result Of The Trust Transaction And How I Am Handling The Result: _____.

I Wish I Can Tell Someone The Truth About....

Ten Truths I Look Forward To Telling Someone....

1.

2.

3.

4.

5.

6.

7.

8.

9.

10.

Date: _____   Mood: _____

Today I Am Taking A Leap Of Faith By:	I Believe:
What I Trust God To Do Today:	I Trust Myself To:
I Feel Free In Letting Go Of The Fear Of:	An Example Of Something That I Rely On Everyday That I Trust:
Something That Didn't Work Out For Me Yesterday That I Am Okay With:	It's Okay That I Cannot Control:
I Am Deciding That My Past Will No Longer Dictate:	Today's Pending Trust Transaction (Between You And Someone Else Where Both Of You Must Trust Each Other With Something Big And/Or Small):

Fill In At Night

The Result Of The Trust Transaction And How I Am Handling The Result: _____.

The Truth
Is I Am
Learning
To Trust
Myself.

Date: _____   Mood: _____

Today I Am Taking A Leap Of Faith By:	I Believe:
What I Trust God To Do Today:	I Trust Myself To:
I Feel Free In Letting Go Of The Fear Of:	An Example Of Something That I Rely On Everyday That I Trust:
Something That Didn't Work Out For Me Yesterday That I Am Okay With:	It's Okay That I Cannot Control:
I Am Deciding That My Past Will No Longer Dictate:	Today's Pending Trust Transaction (Between You And Someone Else Where Both Of You Must Trust Each Other With Something Big And/Or Small):

Fill In At Night

The Result Of The Trust Transaction And How I Am Handling The Result: _____.

In The Past I Have Had Unrealistic Expectations Of....

My Trust & Truth Notes

Trust & Truth

Date: _____   Mood: _____

Today I Am Taking A Leap Of Faith By:	I Believe:
What I Trust God To Do Today:	I Trust Myself To:
I Feel Free In Letting Go Of The Fear Of:	An Example Of Something That I Rely On Everyday That I Trust:
Something That Didn't Work Out For Me Yesterday That I Am Okay With:	It's Okay That I Cannot Control:
I Am Deciding That My Past Will No Longer Dictate:	Today's Pending Trust Transaction (Between You And Someone Else Where Both Of You Must Trust Each Other With Something Big And/Or Small):

Fill In At Night

The Result Of The Trust Transaction And How I Am Handling The Result: _____.

Date: Mood:

Today I Am Taking A Leap Of Faith By: | I Believe:

What I Trust God To Do Today: | I Trust Myself To:

I Feel Free In Letting Go Of The Fear Of: | An Example Of Something That I Rely On Everyday That I Trust:

Something That Didn't Work Out For Me Yesterday That I Am Okay With: | It's Okay That I Cannot Control:

I Am Deciding That My Past Will No Longer Dictate: | Today's Pending Trust Transaction (Between You And Someone Else Where Both Of You Must Trust Each Other With Something Big And/Or Small):

The Result Of The Trust Transaction And How I Am Handling The Result: _____.

Trust & Truth

Date: _____   Mood: _____

Today I Am Taking A Leap Of Faith By:	I Believe:
What I Trust God To Do Today:	I Trust Myself To:
I Feel Free In Letting Go Of The Fear Of:	An Example Of Something That I Rely On Everyday That I Trust:
Something That Didn't Work Out For Me Yesterday That I Am Okay With:	It's Okay That I Cannot Control:
I Am Deciding That My Past Will No Longer Dictate:	Today's Pending Trust Transaction (Between You And Someone Else Where Both Of You Must Trust Each Other With Something Big And/Or Small):

The Result Of The Trust Transaction And How I Am Handling The Result: _____.

Trust & Truth

Date: Mood:

Today I Am Taking A Leap Of Faith By: | I Believe:

What I Trust God To Do Today: | I Trust Myself To:

I Feel Free In Letting Go Of The Fear Of: | An Example Of Something That I Rely On Everyday That I Trust:

Something That Didn't Work Out For Me Yesterday That I Am Okay With: | It's Okay That I Cannot Control:

I Am Deciding That My Past Will No Longer Dictate: | Today's Pending Trust Transaction (Between You And Someone Else Where Both Of You Must Trust Each Other With Something Big And/Or Small):

Fill In At Night

The Result Of The Trust Transaction And How I Am Handling The Result: _____.

I Stopped
Holding On
When I
Realized
It Took Less
Energy To
Let Go.

Seven Truths I Am Happy To Know....

1.

2.

3.

4.

5.

6.

7.

Date: Mood:

Today I Am Taking A Leap Of Faith By:	I Believe:
What I Trust God To Do Today:	I Trust Myself To:
I Feel Free In Letting Go Of The Fear Of:	An Example Of Something That I Rely On Everyday That I Trust:
Something That Didn't Work Out For Me Yesterday That I Am Okay With:	It's Okay That I Cannot Control:
I Am Deciding That My Past Will No Longer Dictate:	Today's Pending Trust Transaction (Between You And Someone Else Where Both Of You Must Trust Each Other With Something Big And/Or Small):

Fill In At Night

The Result Of The Trust Transaction And How I Am Handling The Result: _____.

Date: _____   Mood: _____

Today I Am Taking A Leap Of Faith By:	I Believe:
What I Trust God To Do Today:	I Trust Myself To:
I Feel Free In Letting Go Of The Fear Of:	An Example Of Something That I Rely On Everyday That I Trust:
Something That Didn't Work Out For Me Yesterday That I Am Okay With:	It's Okay That I Cannot Control:
I Am Deciding That My Past Will No Longer Dictate:	Today's Pending Trust Transaction (Between You And Someone Else Where Both Of You Must Trust Each Other With Something Big And/Or Small):

Fill In At Night

The Result Of The Trust Transaction And How I Am Handling The Result: _____.

Date: Mood:

Today I Am Taking A Leap Of Faith By:	I Believe:
What I Trust God To Do Today:	I Trust Myself To:
I Feel Free In Letting Go Of The Fear Of:	An Example Of Something That I Rely On Everyday That I Trust:
Something That Didn't Work Out For Me Yesterday That I Am Okay With:	It's Okay That I Cannot Control:
I Am Deciding That My Past Will No Longer Dictate:	Today's Pending Trust Transaction (Between You And Someone Else Where Both Of You Must Trust Each Other With Something Big And/Or Small):

Fill In At Night

The Result Of The Trust Transaction And How I Am Handling The Result: _____.

Date: Mood:

Today I Am Taking A Leap Of Faith By: | I Believe:

What I Trust God To Do Today: | I Trust Myself To:

I Feel Free In Letting Go Of The Fear Of: | An Example Of Something That I Rely On Everyday That I Trust:

Something That Didn't Work Out For Me Yesterday That I Am Okay With: | It's Okay That I Cannot Control:

I Am Deciding That My Past Will No Longer Dictate: | Today's Pending Trust Transaction (Between You And Someone Else Where Both Of You Must Trust Each Other With Something Big And/Or Small):

Fill In At Night

The Result Of The Trust Transaction And How I Am Handling The Result: _____.

I Will Not Allow My Present To Suffer From Past Beliefs.

Trust & Truth

Date: Mood:

Today I Am Taking A Leap Of Faith By:	I Believe:
What I Trust God To Do Today:	I Trust Myself To:
I Feel Free In Letting Go Of The Fear Of:	An Example Of Something That I Rely On Everyday That I Trust:
Something That Didn't Work Out For Me Yesterday That I Am Okay With:	It's Okay That I Cannot Control:
I Am Deciding That My Past Will No Longer Dictate:	Today's Pending Trust Transaction (Between You And Someone Else Where Both Of You Must Trust Each Other With Something Big And/Or Small):

Fill In At Night

The Result Of The Trust Transaction And How I Am Handling The Result: _____.

Blessed Are Those Who Have Not Seen And Yet Have Believed.

-John 20:29

My Trust & Truth Notes

Trust & Truth

Date: Mood:

Today I Am Taking A Leap Of Faith By: | I Believe:

What I Trust God To Do Today: | I Trust Myself To:

I Feel Free In Letting Go Of The Fear | An Example Of Something That I Rely On
Of: | Everyday That I Trust:

Something That Didn't Work Out For | It's Okay That I Cannot Control:
Me Yesterday That I Am Okay With: |

I Am Deciding That My Past Will No | Today's Pending Trust Transaction
Longer Dictate: | (Between You And Someone Else Where
                                       | Both Of You Must Trust Each Other With
                                       | Something Big And/Or Small):

Fill In At Night

The Result Of The Trust Transaction And How I Am Handling The Result: _____.

Date: _____   Mood: _____

Today I Am Taking A Leap Of Faith By:	I Believe:
What I Trust God To Do Today:	I Trust Myself To:
I Feel Free In Letting Go Of The Fear Of:	An Example Of Something That I Rely On Everyday That I Trust:
Something That Didn't Work Out For Me Yesterday That I Am Okay With:	It's Okay That I Cannot Control:
I Am Deciding That My Past Will No Longer Dictate:	Today's Pending Trust Transaction (Between You And Someone Else Where Both Of You Must Trust Each Other With Something Big And/Or Small):

Fill In At Night

The Result Of The Trust Transaction And How I Am Handling The Result: _____.

Trust & Truth

Date: Mood:

Today I Am Taking A Leap Of Faith By: I Believe:

What I Trust God To Do Today: I Trust Myself To:

I Feel Free In Letting Go Of The Fear   An Example Of Something That I Rely On
Of: Everyday That I Trust:

Something That Didn't Work Out For   It's Okay That I Cannot Control:
Me Yesterday That I Am Okay With:

I Am Deciding That My Past Will No   Today's Pending Trust Transaction
Longer Dictate: (Between You And Someone Else Where
                                         Both Of You Must Trust Each Other With
                                         Something Big And/Or Small):

Fill In At Night

The Result Of The Trust Transaction And How I Am Handling The Result: _____.

Date: Mood:

Today I Am Taking A Leap Of Faith By: | I Believe:

What I Trust God To Do Today: | I Trust Myself To:

I Feel Free In Letting Go Of The Fear Of: | An Example Of Something That I Rely On Everyday That I Trust:

Something That Didn't Work Out For Me Yesterday That I Am Okay With: | It's Okay That I Cannot Control:

I Am Deciding That My Past Will No Longer Dictate: | Today's Pending Trust Transaction (Between You And Someone Else Where Both Of You Must Trust Each Other With Something Big And/Or Small):

Fill In At Night

The Result Of The Trust Transaction And How I Am Handling The Result: _____.

I Will Not
Buy Into
A Lie Just
Because
My Heart
Is Hungry.

I Show Others That I Am Dependable By....

Trust & Truth

Date: _____   Mood: _____

Today I Am Taking A Leap Of Faith By: I Believe:

What I Trust God To Do Today: I Trust Myself To:

I Feel Free In Letting Go Of The Fear Of: An Example Of Something That I Rely On Everyday That I Trust:

Something That Didn't Work Out For Me Yesterday That I Am Okay With: It's Okay That I Cannot Control:

I Am Deciding That My Past Will No Longer Dictate: Today's Pending Trust Transaction (Between You And Someone Else Where Both Of You Must Trust Each Other With Something Big And/Or Small):

Fill In At Night

The Result Of The Trust Transaction And How I Am Handling The Result: _____.

Trust & Truth

Date: _____ Mood: _____

Today I Am Taking A Leap Of Faith By:	I Believe:
What I Trust God To Do Today:	I Trust Myself To:
I Feel Free In Letting Go Of The Fear Of:	An Example Of Something That I Rely On Everyday That I Trust:
Something That Didn't Work Out For Me Yesterday That I Am Okay With:	It's Okay That I Cannot Control:
I Am Deciding That My Past Will No Longer Dictate:	Today's Pending Trust Transaction (Between You And Someone Else Where Both Of You Must Trust Each Other With Something Big And/Or Small):

Fill In At Night

The Result Of The Trust Transaction And How I Am Handling The Result: _____.

Truth

+

Transparency

=

Trust

I Pay Attention To....

Trust & Truth

Date: _____   Mood: _____

Today I Am Taking A Leap Of Faith By: | **I Believe:**

What I Trust God To Do Today: | **I Trust Myself To:**

I Feel Free In Letting Go Of The Fear Of: | **An Example Of Something That I Rely On Everyday That I Trust:**

Something That Didn't Work Out For Me Yesterday That I Am Okay With: | **It's Okay That I Cannot Control:**

I Am Deciding That My Past Will No Longer Dictate: | **Today's Pending Trust Transaction (Between You And Someone Else Where Both Of You Must Trust Each Other With Something Big And/Or Small):**

Fill In At Night

The Result Of The Trust Transaction And How I Am Handling The Result: _____.

My Past Decisions Have Taught Me How to Make Better Decisions That Won't Isolate Me From A Wonderful Future.

To Heal
A Wound
We Must
Forgive What
Caused It.

Trust & Truth

Date: _____   Mood: _____

Today I Am Taking A Leap Of Faith By:	I Believe:
What I Trust God To Do Today:	I Trust Myself To:
I Feel Free In Letting Go Of The Fear Of:	An Example Of Something That I Rely On Everyday That I Trust:
Something That Didn't Work Out For Me Yesterday That I Am Okay With:	It's Okay That I Cannot Control:
I Am Deciding That My Past Will No Longer Dictate:	Today's Pending Trust Transaction (Between You And Someone Else Where Both Of You Must Trust Each Other With Something Big And/Or Small):

Fill In At Night

The Result Of The Trust Transaction And How I Am Handling The Result: _____.

Trust & Truth

Date: _____   Mood: _____

Today I Am Taking A Leap Of Faith By: **I Believe:**

What I Trust God To Do Today: **I Trust Myself To:**

I Feel Free In Letting Go Of The Fear Of: **An Example Of Something That I Rely On Everyday That I Trust:**

Something That Didn't Work Out For Me Yesterday That I Am Okay With: **It's Okay That I Cannot Control:**

I Am Deciding That My Past Will No Longer Dictate: **Today's Pending Trust Transaction (Between You And Someone Else Where Both Of You Must Trust Each Other With Something Big And/Or Small):**

Fill In At Night

The Result Of The Trust Transaction And How I Am Handling The Result: _____.

Date: _____   Mood: _____

Today I Am Taking A Leap Of Faith By:	I Believe:
What I Trust God To Do Today:	I Trust Myself To:
I Feel Free In Letting Go Of The Fear Of:	An Example Of Something That I Rely On Everyday That I Trust:
Something That Didn't Work Out For Me Yesterday That I Am Okay With:	It's Okay That I Cannot Control:
I Am Deciding That My Past Will No Longer Dictate:	Today's Pending Trust Transaction (Between You And Someone Else Where Both Of You Must Trust Each Other With Something Big And/Or Small):

Fill In At Night

The Result Of The Trust Transaction And How I Am Handling The Result: _____.

Letting Go Of Those I Can't Trust.

Date: Mood:

Today I Am Taking A Leap Of Faith By:	I Believe:
What I Trust God To Do Today:	I Trust Myself To:
I Feel Free In Letting Go Of The Fear Of:	An Example Of Something That I Rely On Everyday That I Trust:
Something That Didn't Work Out For Me Yesterday That I Am Okay With:	It's Okay That I Cannot Control:
I Am Deciding That My Past Will No Longer Dictate:	Today's Pending Trust Transaction (Between You And Someone Else Where Both Of You Must Trust Each Other With Something Big And/Or Small):

Fill In At Night

The Result Of The Trust Transaction And How I Am Handling The Result: _____.

There Is A Beautiful Beginning That Has Come After That Hurtful End. I'm Excited.

Date: _____   Mood: _____

Today I Am Taking A Leap Of Faith By:	I Believe:
What I Trust God To Do Today:	I Trust Myself To:
I Feel Free In Letting Go Of The Fear Of:	An Example Of Something That I Rely On Everyday That I Trust:
Something That Didn't Work Out For Me Yesterday That I Am Okay With:	It's Okay That I Cannot Control:
I Am Deciding That My Past Will No Longer Dictate:	Today's Pending Trust Transaction (Between You And Someone Else Where Both Of You Must Trust Each Other With Something Big And/Or Small):

Fill In At Night

The Result Of The Trust Transaction And How I Am Handling The Result: _____.

Date: Mood:

Today I Am Taking A Leap Of Faith By:	I Believe:
What I Trust God To Do Today:	I Trust Myself To:
I Feel Free In Letting Go Of The Fear Of:	An Example Of Something That I Rely On Everyday That I Trust:
Something That Didn't Work Out For Me Yesterday That I Am Okay With:	It's Okay That I Cannot Control:
I Am Deciding That My Past Will No Longer Dictate:	Today's Pending Trust Transaction (Between You And Someone Else Where Both Of You Must Trust Each Other With Something Big And/Or Small):

Fill In At Night

The Result Of The Trust Transaction And How I Am Handling The Result: _____.

Trust & Truth

Date: _____   Mood: _____

Today I Am Taking A Leap Of Faith By:	I Believe:
What I Trust God To Do Today:	I Trust Myself To:
I Feel Free In Letting Go Of The Fear Of:	An Example Of Something That I Rely On Everyday That I Trust:
Something That Didn't Work Out For Me Yesterday That I Am Okay With:	It's Okay That I Cannot Control:
I Am Deciding That My Past Will No Longer Dictate:	Today's Pending Trust Transaction (Between You And Someone Else Where Both Of You Must Trust Each Other With Something Big And/Or Small):

Fill In At Night

The Result Of The Trust Transaction And How I Am Handling The Result: _____.

Trust & Truth

Date: _____   Mood: _____

Today I Am Taking A Leap Of Faith By:	I Believe:
What I Trust God To Do Today:	I Trust Myself To:
I Feel Free In Letting Go Of The Fear Of:	An Example Of Something That I Rely On Everyday That I Trust:
Something That Didn't Work Out For Me Yesterday That I Am Okay With:	It's Okay That I Cannot Control:
I Am Deciding That My Past Will No Longer Dictate:	Today's Pending Trust Transaction (Between You And Someone Else Where Both Of You Must Trust Each Other With Something Big And/Or Small):

Fill In At Night

The Result Of The Trust Transaction And How I Am Handling The Result: _____.

The Commitment I Am Making To Myself....

Trust & Truth

Date: _____   Mood: _____

Today I Am Taking A Leap Of Faith By:	I Believe:
What I Trust God To Do Today:	I Trust Myself To:
I Feel Free In Letting Go Of The Fear Of:	An Example Of Something That I Rely On Everyday That I Trust:
Something That Didn't Work Out For Me Yesterday That I Am Okay With:	It's Okay That I Cannot Control:
I Am Deciding That My Past Will No Longer Dictate:	Today's Pending Trust Transaction (Between You And Someone Else Where Both Of You Must Trust Each Other With Something Big And/Or Small):

Fill In At Night

The Result Of The Trust Transaction And How I Am Handling The Result: _____.

My Trust & Truth Notes

Date: _____   Mood: _____

Today I Am Taking A Leap Of Faith By:	I Believe:
What I Trust God To Do Today:	I Trust Myself To:
I Feel Free In Letting Go Of The Fear Of:	An Example Of Something That I Rely On Everyday That I Trust:
Something That Didn't Work Out For Me Yesterday That I Am Okay With:	It's Okay That I Cannot Control:
I Am Deciding That My Past Will No Longer Dictate:	Today's Pending Trust Transaction (Between You And Someone Else Where Both Of You Must Trust Each Other With Something Big And/Or Small):

Fill In At Night

The Result Of The Trust Transaction And How I Am Handling The Result: _____.

Trust & Truth

Date: _____   Mood: _____

Today I Am Taking A Leap Of Faith By:	I Believe:
What I Trust God To Do Today:	I Trust Myself To:
I Feel Free In Letting Go Of The Fear Of:	An Example Of Something That I Rely On Everyday That I Trust:
Something That Didn't Work Out For Me Yesterday That I Am Okay With:	It's Okay That I Cannot Control:
I Am Deciding That My Past Will No Longer Dictate:	Today's Pending Trust Transaction (Between You And Someone Else Where Both Of You Must Trust Each Other With Something Big And/Or Small):

Fill In At Night

The Result Of The Trust Transaction And How I Am Handling The Result: _____.

Trust & Truth

Date: _____   Mood: _____

Today I Am Taking A Leap Of Faith By:	I Believe:
What I Trust God To Do Today:	I Trust Myself To:
I Feel Free In Letting Go Of The Fear Of:	An Example Of Something That I Rely On Everyday That I Trust:
Something That Didn't Work Out For Me Yesterday That I Am Okay With:	It's Okay That I Cannot Control:
I Am Deciding That My Past Will No Longer Dictate:	Today's Pending Trust Transaction (Between You And Someone Else Where Both Of You Must Trust Each Other With Something Big And/Or Small):

Fill In At Night

The Result Of The Trust Transaction And How I Am Handling The Result: _____.

I Don't
Just Trust
Actions,
I Trust
Consistency
In Actions.

My Spirit
Guides Me

From

Crucial

Mistakes.

Date: _____   Mood: _____

Today I Am Taking A Leap Of Faith By:	I Believe:
What I Trust God To Do Today:	I Trust Myself To:
I Feel Free In Letting Go Of The Fear Of:	An Example Of Something That I Rely On Everyday That I Trust:
Something That Didn't Work Out For Me Yesterday That I Am Okay With:	It's Okay That I Cannot Control:
I Am Deciding That My Past Will No Longer Dictate:	Today's Pending Trust Transaction (Between You And Someone Else Where Both Of You Must Trust Each Other With Something Big And/Or Small):

Fill In At Night

The Result Of The Trust Transaction And How I Am Handling The Result: _____.

Trust & Truth

Date: | Mood:

Today I Am Taking A Leap Of Faith By: | **I Believe:**

What I Trust God To Do Today: | **I Trust Myself To:**

I Feel Free In Letting Go Of The Fear Of: | **An Example Of Something That I Rely On Everyday That I Trust:**

Something That Didn't Work Out For Me Yesterday That I Am Okay With: | **It's Okay That I Cannot Control:**

I Am Deciding That My Past Will No Longer Dictate: | **Today's Pending Trust Transaction (Between You And Someone Else Where Both Of You Must Trust Each Other With Something Big And/Or Small):**

Fill In At Night

The Result Of The Trust Transaction And How I Am Handling The Result: _____.

Date: Mood:

Today I Am Taking A Leap Of Faith By: I Believe:

What I Trust God To Do Today: I Trust Myself To:

I Feel Free In Letting Go Of The Fear   An Example Of Something That I Rely On
Of: Everyday That I Trust:

Something That Didn't Work Out For   It's Okay That I Cannot Control:
Me Yesterday That I Am Okay With:

I Am Deciding That My Past Will No   Today's Pending Trust Transaction
Longer Dictate: (Between You And Someone Else Where
                                         Both Of You Must Trust Each Other With
                                         Something Big And/Or Small):

Fill In At Night

The Result Of The Trust Transaction And How I Am Handling The Result: _____.

Trust & Truth

Date: Mood:

Today I Am Taking A Leap Of Faith By: | I Believe:

What I Trust God To Do Today: | I Trust Myself To:

I Feel Free In Letting Go Of The Fear | An Example Of Something That I Rely On
Of: | Everyday That I Trust:

Something That Didn't Work Out For | It's Okay That I Cannot Control:
Me Yesterday That I Am Okay With: |

I Am Deciding That My Past Will No | Today's Pending Trust Transaction
Longer Dictate: | (Between You And Someone Else Where
                                         | Both Of You Must Trust Each Other With
                                         | Something Big And/Or Small):

Fill In At Night

The Result Of The Trust Transaction And How I Am Handling The Result: _____.

I Am Letting Go Of The Need To Control....

Trust & Truth

Date: Mood:

Today I Am Taking A Leap Of Faith By:	I Believe:
What I Trust God To Do Today:	I Trust Myself To:
I Feel Free In Letting Go Of The Fear Of:	An Example Of Something That I Rely On Everyday That I Trust:
Something That Didn't Work Out For Me Yesterday That I Am Okay With:	It's Okay That I Cannot Control:
I Am Deciding That My Past Will No Longer Dictate:	Today's Pending Trust Transaction (Between You And Someone Else Where Both Of You Must Trust Each Other With Something Big And/Or Small):

Fill In At Night

The Result Of The Trust Transaction And How I Am Handling The Result: _____.

Date: _____   Mood: _____

Today I Am Taking A Leap Of Faith By:	I Believe:
What I Trust God To Do Today:	I Trust Myself To:
I Feel Free In Letting Go Of The Fear Of:	An Example Of Something That I Rely On Everyday That I Trust:
Something That Didn't Work Out For Me Yesterday That I Am Okay With:	It's Okay That I Cannot Control:
I Am Deciding That My Past Will No Longer Dictate:	Today's Pending Trust Transaction (Between You And Someone Else Where Both Of You Must Trust Each Other With Something Big And/Or Small):

Fill In At Night

The Result Of The Trust Transaction And How I Am Handling The Result: _____.

Date: _____   Mood: _____

Today I Am Taking A Leap Of Faith By:	I Believe:
What I Trust God To Do Today:	I Trust Myself To:
I Feel Free In Letting Go Of The Fear Of:	An Example Of Something That I Rely On Everyday That I Trust:
Something That Didn't Work Out For Me Yesterday That I Am Okay With:	It's Okay That I Cannot Control:
I Am Deciding That My Past Will No Longer Dictate:	Today's Pending Trust Transaction (Between You And Someone Else Where Both Of You Must Trust Each Other With Something Big And/Or Small):

Fill In At Night

The Result Of The Trust Transaction And How I Am Handling The Result: _____.

I Trust In God
to Make My
Dreams Come
True Through
People Who
I May Have
Never Expected.

I May No
Longer Want
to Trust That
Person But I
Will Forever
Trust In Love.

Date: _____   Mood: _____

Today I Am Taking A Leap Of Faith By: | I Believe:

What I Trust God To Do Today: | I Trust Myself To:

I Feel Free In Letting Go Of The Fear Of: | An Example Of Something That I Rely On Everyday That I Trust:

Something That Didn't Work Out For Me Yesterday That I Am Okay With: | It's Okay That I Cannot Control:

I Am Deciding That My Past Will No Longer Dictate: | Today's Pending Trust Transaction (Between You And Someone Else Where Both Of You Must Trust Each Other With Something Big And/Or Small):

Fill In At Night

The Result Of The Trust Transaction And How I Am Handling The Result: _____.

Trust & Truth

Date: _____   Mood: _____

Today I Am Taking A Leap Of Faith By:	I Believe:
What I Trust God To Do Today:	I Trust Myself To:
I Feel Free In Letting Go Of The Fear Of:	An Example Of Something That I Rely On Everyday That I Trust:
Something That Didn't Work Out For Me Yesterday That I Am Okay With:	It's Okay That I Cannot Control:
I Am Deciding That My Past Will No Longer Dictate:	Today's Pending Trust Transaction (Between You And Someone Else Where Both Of You Must Trust Each Other With Something Big And/Or Small):

Fill In At Night

The Result Of The Trust Transaction And How I Am Handling The Result: _____.

Trust & Truth

Date: _____   Mood: _____

Today I Am Taking A Leap Of Faith By:	I Believe:
What I Trust God To Do Today:	I Trust Myself To:
I Feel Free In Letting Go Of The Fear Of:	An Example Of Something That I Rely On Everyday That I Trust:
Something That Didn't Work Out For Me Yesterday That I Am Okay With:	It's Okay That I Cannot Control:
I Am Deciding That My Past Will No Longer Dictate:	Today's Pending Trust Transaction (Between You And Someone Else Where Both Of You Must Trust Each Other With Something Big And/Or Small):

Fill In At Night

The Result Of The Trust Transaction And How I Am Handling The Result: _____.

My Trust & Truth Notes

The Best
Evidence
Of Love
Is
Trust.

I Let Go
So I Can
Accept The
Good That Is
Coming Into
My Life.

Trust & Truth

Date: _____   Mood: _____

Today I Am Taking A Leap Of Faith By: **I Believe:**

What I Trust God To Do Today: **I Trust Myself To:**

I Feel Free In Letting Go Of The Fear Of: **An Example Of Something That I Rely On Everyday That I Trust:**

Something That Didn't Work Out For Me Yesterday That I Am Okay With: **It's Okay That I Cannot Control:**

I Am Deciding That My Past Will No Longer Dictate: **Today's Pending Trust Transaction (Between You And Someone Else Where Both Of You Must Trust Each Other With Something Big And/Or Small):**

Fill In At Night

The Result Of The Trust Transaction And How I Am Handling The Result: _____.

I Love That My Heart Is....

Date: _____   Mood: _____

Today I Am Taking A Leap Of Faith By:	I Believe:
What I Trust God To Do Today:	I Trust Myself To:
I Feel Free In Letting Go Of The Fear Of:	An Example Of Something That I Rely On Everyday That I Trust:
Something That Didn't Work Out For Me Yesterday That I Am Okay With:	It's Okay That I Cannot Control:
I Am Deciding That My Past Will No Longer Dictate:	Today's Pending Trust Transaction (Between You And Someone Else Where Both Of You Must Trust Each Other With Something Big And/Or Small):

Fill In At Night

The Result Of The Trust Transaction And How I Am Handling The Result: _____.

Trust & Truth

Date: Mood:

Today I Am Taking A Leap Of Faith By: I Believe:

What I Trust God To Do Today: I Trust Myself To:

I Feel Free In Letting Go Of The Fear   An Example Of Something That I Rely On
Of: Everyday That I Trust:

Something That Didn't Work Out For   It's Okay That I Cannot Control:
Me Yesterday That I Am Okay With:

I Am Deciding That My Past Will No   Today's Pending Trust Transaction
Longer Dictate: (Between You And Someone Else Where
                                               Both Of You Must Trust Each Other With
                                               Something Big And/Or Small):

Fill In At Night

The Result Of The Trust Transaction And How I Am Handling The Result: _____.

Date: Mood:

Today I Am Taking A Leap Of Faith By: I Believe:

What I Trust God To Do Today: I Trust Myself To:

I Feel Free In Letting Go Of The Fear   An Example Of Something That I Rely On
Of: Everyday That I Trust:

Something That Didn't Work Out For   It's Okay That I Cannot Control:
Me Yesterday That I Am Okay With:

I Am Deciding That My Past Will No   Today's Pending Trust Transaction
Longer Dictate: (Between You And Someone Else Where
                                          Both Of You Must Trust Each Other With
                                          Something Big And/Or Small):

Fill In At Night

The Result Of The Trust Transaction And How I Am Handling The Result: _____.

Date: _____   Mood: _____

Today I Am Taking A Leap Of Faith By:	I Believe:
What I Trust God To Do Today:	I Trust Myself To:
I Feel Free In Letting Go Of The Fear Of:	An Example Of Something That I Rely On Everyday That I Trust:
Something That Didn't Work Out For Me Yesterday That I Am Okay With:	It's Okay That I Cannot Control:
I Am Deciding That My Past Will No Longer Dictate:	Today's Pending Trust Transaction (Between You And Someone Else Where Both Of You Must Trust Each Other With Something Big And/Or Small):

Fill In At Night

The Result Of The Trust Transaction And How I Am Handling The Result: _____.

Trust & Truth

Date: Mood:

Today I Am Taking A Leap Of Faith By: | I Believe:

What I Trust God To Do Today: | I Trust Myself To:

I Feel Free In Letting Go Of The Fear Of: | An Example Of Something That I Rely On Everyday That I Trust:

Something That Didn't Work Out For Me Yesterday That I Am Okay With: | It's Okay That I Cannot Control:

I Am Deciding That My Past Will No Longer Dictate: | Today's Pending Trust Transaction (Between You And Someone Else Where Both Of You Must Trust Each Other With Something Big And/Or Small):

Fill In At Night

The Result Of The Trust Transaction And How I Am Handling The Result: _____.

Date: _____   Mood: _____

Today I Am Taking A Leap Of Faith By:	I Believe:
What I Trust God To Do Today:	I Trust Myself To:
I Feel Free In Letting Go Of The Fear Of:	An Example Of Something That I Rely On Everyday That I Trust:
Something That Didn't Work Out For Me Yesterday That I Am Okay With:	It's Okay That I Cannot Control:
I Am Deciding That My Past Will No Longer Dictate:	Today's Pending Trust Transaction (Between You And Someone Else Where Both Of You Must Trust Each Other With Something Big And/Or Small):

Fill In At Night

The Result Of The Trust Transaction And How I Am Handling The Result: _____.

Date: Mood:

Today I Am Taking A Leap Of Faith By: I Believe:

What I Trust God To Do Today: I Trust Myself To:

I Feel Free In Letting Go Of The Fear Of: An Example Of Something That I Rely On Everyday That I Trust:

Something That Didn't Work Out For Me Yesterday That I Am Okay With: It's Okay That I Cannot Control:

I Am Deciding That My Past Will No Longer Dictate: Today's Pending Trust Transaction (Between You And Someone Else Where Both Of You Must Trust Each Other With Something Big And/Or Small):

Fill In At Night

The Result Of The Trust Transaction And How I Am Handling The Result: _____.

Trust & Truth

Date: _____   Mood: _____

Today I Am Taking A Leap Of Faith By:

I Believe:

What I Trust God To Do Today:

I Trust Myself To:

I Feel Free In Letting Go Of The Fear Of:

An Example Of Something That I Rely On Everyday That I Trust:

Something That Didn't Work Out For Me Yesterday That I Am Okay With:

It's Okay That I Cannot Control:

I Am Deciding That My Past Will No Longer Dictate:

Today's Pending Trust Transaction (Between You And Someone Else Where Both Of You Must Trust Each Other With Something Big And/Or Small):

Fill In At Night

The Result Of The Trust Transaction And How I Am Handling The Result: _____.

My Trust & Truth Notes

Trust & Truth

Date: _____   Mood: _____

Today I Am Taking A Leap Of Faith By:	I Believe:
What I Trust God To Do Today:	I Trust Myself To:
I Feel Free In Letting Go Of The Fear Of:	An Example Of Something That I Rely On Everyday That I Trust:
Something That Didn't Work Out For Me Yesterday That I Am Okay With:	It's Okay That I Cannot Control:
I Am Deciding That My Past Will No Longer Dictate:	Today's Pending Trust Transaction (Between You And Someone Else Where Both Of You Must Trust Each Other With Something Big And/Or Small):

Fill In At Night

The Result Of The Trust Transaction And How I Am Handling The Result: _____.

Trust & Truth

Date: _____   Mood: _____

Today I Am Taking A Leap Of Faith By:	I Believe:
What I Trust God To Do Today:	I Trust Myself To:
I Feel Free In Letting Go Of The Fear Of:	An Example Of Something That I Rely On Everyday That I Trust:
Something That Didn't Work Out For Me Yesterday That I Am Okay With:	It's Okay That I Cannot Control:
I Am Deciding That My Past Will No Longer Dictate:	Today's Pending Trust Transaction (Between You And Someone Else Where Both Of You Must Trust Each Other With Something Big And/Or Small):

Fill In At Night

The Result Of The Trust Transaction And How I Am Handling The Result: _____.

Trust & Truth

Date: _____   Mood: _____

Today I Am Taking A Leap Of Faith By:	I Believe:
What I Trust God To Do Today:	I Trust Myself To:
I Feel Free In Letting Go Of The Fear Of:	An Example Of Something That I Rely On Everyday That I Trust:
Something That Didn't Work Out For Me Yesterday That I Am Okay With:	It's Okay That I Cannot Control:
I Am Deciding That My Past Will No Longer Dictate:	Today's Pending Trust Transaction (Between You And Someone Else Where Both Of You Must Trust Each Other With Something Big And/Or Small):

Fill In At Night

The Result Of The Trust Transaction And How I Am Handling The Result: _____.

I Believe
In Second
Chances
Even
Though Not
Everyone
Deserves
Them.

Working On
Forgiving
Others As
Quickly As I
Would Like
God To Forgive
Me.

Date: Mood:

Today I Am Taking A Leap Of Faith By:	I Believe:
What I Trust God To Do Today:	I Trust Myself To:
I Feel Free In Letting Go Of The Fear Of:	An Example Of Something That I Rely On Everyday That I Trust:
Something That Didn't Work Out For Me Yesterday That I Am Okay With:	It's Okay That I Cannot Control:
I Am Deciding That My Past Will No Longer Dictate:	Today's Pending Trust Transaction (Between You And Someone Else Where Both Of You Must Trust Each Other With Something Big And/Or Small):

Fill In At Night

The Result Of The Trust Transaction And How I Am Handling The Result: _____.

I Want To Build Trust Because....

Trust & Truth

Date: _____   Mood: _____

Today I Am Taking A Leap Of Faith By:	I Believe:
What I Trust God To Do Today:	I Trust Myself To:
I Feel Free In Letting Go Of The Fear Of:	An Example Of Something That I Rely On Everyday That I Trust:
Something That Didn't Work Out For Me Yesterday That I Am Okay With:	It's Okay That I Cannot Control:
I Am Deciding That My Past Will No Longer Dictate:	Today's Pending Trust Transaction (Between You And Someone Else Where Both Of You Must Trust Each Other With Something Big And/Or Small):

Fill In At Night

The Result Of The Trust Transaction And How I Am Handling The Result: _____.

No Longer

Allowing

One Person's

Mistake To

Be The Reason

Why I Won't

Trust Anyone.

Date: Mood:

Today I Am Taking A Leap Of Faith By: | I Believe:

What I Trust God To Do Today: | I Trust Myself To:

I Feel Free In Letting Go Of The Fear Of: | An Example Of Something That I Rely On Everyday That I Trust:

Something That Didn't Work Out For Me Yesterday That I Am Okay With: | It's Okay That I Cannot Control:

I Am Deciding That My Past Will No Longer Dictate: | Today's Pending Trust Transaction (Between You And Someone Else Where Both Of You Must Trust Each Other With Something Big And/Or Small):

Fill In At Night

The Result Of The Trust Transaction And How I Am Handling The Result: _____.

Regardless Of
How Many Times
I Fall, I Trust
Myself To Get
Up Again And
Stand Stronger.

Date: Mood:

Today I Am Taking A Leap Of Faith By:	I Believe:
What I Trust God To Do Today:	I Trust Myself To:
I Feel Free In Letting Go Of The Fear Of:	An Example Of Something That I Rely On Everyday That I Trust:
Something That Didn't Work Out For Me Yesterday That I Am Okay With:	It's Okay That I Cannot Control:
I Am Deciding That My Past Will No Longer Dictate:	Today's Pending Trust Transaction (Between You And Someone Else Where Both Of You Must Trust Each Other With Something Big And/Or Small):

Fill In At Night

The Result Of The Trust Transaction And How I Am Handling The Result: _____.

Trust & Truth

Date: Mood:

Today I Am Taking A Leap Of Faith By: | I Believe:

What I Trust God To Do Today: I Trust Myself To:

I Feel Free In Letting Go Of The Fear   An Example Of Something That I Rely On
Of: Everyday That I Trust:

Something That Didn't Work Out For   It's Okay That I Cannot Control:
Me Yesterday That I Am Okay With:

I Am Deciding That My Past Will No   Today's Pending Trust Transaction
Longer Dictate: (Between You And Someone Else Where
                                                             Both Of You Must Trust Each Other With
                                                             Something Big And/Or Small):

Fill In At Night

The Result Of The Trust Transaction And How I Am Handling The Result: _____.

My Trust & Truth Notes

I Believe In Myself Enough To Let Go Of Your Lies.

Date: _____   Mood: _____

Today I Am Taking A Leap Of Faith By:	I Believe:
What I Trust God To Do Today:	I Trust Myself To:
I Feel Free In Letting Go Of The Fear Of:	An Example Of Something That I Rely On Everyday That I Trust:
Something That Didn't Work Out For Me Yesterday That I Am Okay With:	It's Okay That I Cannot Control:
I Am Deciding That My Past Will No Longer Dictate:	Today's Pending Trust Transaction (Between You And Someone Else Where Both Of You Must Trust Each Other With Something Big And/Or Small):

Fill In At Night

The Result Of The Trust Transaction And How I Am Handling The Result: _____.

Date: _____   Mood: _____

Today I Am Taking A Leap Of Faith By:	I Believe:
What I Trust God To Do Today:	I Trust Myself To:
I Feel Free In Letting Go Of The Fear Of:	An Example Of Something That I Rely On Everyday That I Trust:
Something That Didn't Work Out For Me Yesterday That I Am Okay With:	It's Okay That I Cannot Control:
I Am Deciding That My Past Will No Longer Dictate:	Today's Pending Trust Transaction (Between You And Someone Else Where Both Of You Must Trust Each Other With Something Big And/Or Small):

Fill In At Night

The Result Of The Trust Transaction And How I Am Handling The Result: _____.

Date: _____   Mood: _____

Today I Am Taking A Leap Of Faith By: | **I Believe:**

What I Trust God To Do Today: | **I Trust Myself To:**

I Feel Free In Letting Go Of The Fear Of: | **An Example Of Something That I Rely On Everyday That I Trust:**

Something That Didn't Work Out For Me Yesterday That I Am Okay With: | **It's Okay That I Cannot Control:**

I Am Deciding That My Past Will No Longer Dictate: | **Today's Pending Trust Transaction (Between You And Someone Else Where Both Of You Must Trust Each Other With Something Big And/Or Small):**

Fill In At Night

The Result Of The Trust Transaction And How I Am Handling The Result: _____.

Trust & Truth

Date: Mood:

Today I Am Taking A Leap Of Faith By: | I Believe:

What I Trust God To Do Today: | I Trust Myself To:

I Feel Free In Letting Go Of The Fear Of: | An Example Of Something That I Rely On Everyday That I Trust:

Something That Didn't Work Out For Me Yesterday That I Am Okay With: | It's Okay That I Cannot Control:

I Am Deciding That My Past Will No Longer Dictate: | Today's Pending Trust Transaction (Between You And Someone Else Where Both Of You Must Trust Each Other With Something Big And/Or Small):

Fill In At Night

The Result Of The Trust Transaction And How I Am Handling The Result: _____.

Date: _____   Mood: _____

Today I Am Taking A Leap Of Faith By:	I Believe:
What I Trust God To Do Today:	I Trust Myself To:
I Feel Free In Letting Go Of The Fear Of:	An Example Of Something That I Rely On Everyday That I Trust:
Something That Didn't Work Out For Me Yesterday That I Am Okay With:	It's Okay That I Cannot Control:
I Am Deciding That My Past Will No Longer Dictate:	Today's Pending Trust Transaction (Between You And Someone Else Where Both Of You Must Trust Each Other With Something Big And/Or Small):

Fill In At Night

The Result Of The Trust Transaction And How I Am Handling The Result: _____.

I Know The
Difference
Between
Holding On For
Too Long
And Letting Go
Too Easily.

My Trust & Truth Notes

Trust & Truth

Date: _____   Mood: _____

Today I Am Taking A Leap Of Faith By: I Believe:

What I Trust God To Do Today: I Trust Myself To:

I Feel Free In Letting Go Of The Fear   An Example Of Something That I Rely On
Of: Everyday That I Trust:

Something That Didn't Work Out For   It's Okay That I Cannot Control:
Me Yesterday That I Am Okay With:

I Am Deciding That My Past Will No   Today's Pending Trust Transaction
Longer Dictate: (Between You And Someone Else Where
                                           Both Of You Must Trust Each Other With
                                           Something Big And/Or Small):

Fill In At Night

The Result Of The Trust Transaction And How I Am Handling The Result: _____.

Date: Mood:

Today I Am Taking A Leap Of Faith By:	I Believe:
What I Trust God To Do Today:	I Trust Myself To:
I Feel Free In Letting Go Of The Fear Of:	An Example Of Something That I Rely On Everyday That I Trust:
Something That Didn't Work Out For Me Yesterday That I Am Okay With:	It's Okay That I Cannot Control:
I Am Deciding That My Past Will No Longer Dictate:	Today's Pending Trust Transaction (Between You And Someone Else Where Both Of You Must Trust Each Other With Something Big And/Or Small):

Fill In At Night

The Result Of The Trust Transaction And How I Am Handling The Result: _____.

I Let Go Of
All The Hurt
Within Me
Because My
Purpose Is
Bigger Than
My Lack Of
Trust In You.

Date: Mood:

Today I Am Taking A Leap Of Faith By:	I Believe:
What I Trust God To Do Today:	I Trust Myself To:
I Feel Free In Letting Go Of The Fear Of:	An Example Of Something That I Rely On Everyday That I Trust:
Something That Didn't Work Out For Me Yesterday That I Am Okay With:	It's Okay That I Cannot Control:
I Am Deciding That My Past Will No Longer Dictate:	Today's Pending Trust Transaction (Between You And Someone Else Where Both Of You Must Trust Each Other With Something Big And/Or Small):

Fill In At Night

The Result Of The Trust Transaction And How I Am Handling The Result: _____.

Because I
Don't Doubt
My Instincts,
I Don't
Withhold My
Trust To Those
Who Are
Worthy Of It.

Trust & Truth

Date: _____   Mood: _____

Today I Am Taking A Leap Of Faith By:	**I Believe:**
What I Trust God To Do Today:	**I Trust Myself To:**
I Feel Free In Letting Go Of The Fear Of:	**An Example Of Something That I Rely On Everyday That I Trust:**
Something That Didn't Work Out For Me Yesterday That I Am Okay With:	**It's Okay That I Cannot Control:**
I Am Deciding That My Past Will No Longer Dictate:	**Today's Pending Trust Transaction (Between You And Someone Else Where Both Of You Must Trust Each Other With Something Big And/Or Small):**

Fill In At Night

The Result Of The Trust Transaction And How I Am Handling The Result: _____.

My Trust & Truth Notes

It Is Exactly
What I Think
It Is And
I Will Never
Be Upset
For Knowing.

I Will Only
Look At You
With Love Even
When You Choose
To Live In A
Lie. I Will Let
You Move On
Without Me.

Date: _____   Mood: _____

Today I Am Taking A Leap Of Faith By:	I Believe:
What I Trust God To Do Today:	I Trust Myself To:
I Feel Free In Letting Go Of The Fear Of:	An Example Of Something That I Rely On Everyday That I Trust:
Something That Didn't Work Out For Me Yesterday That I Am Okay With:	It's Okay That I Cannot Control:
I Am Deciding That My Past Will No Longer Dictate:	Today's Pending Trust Transaction (Between You And Someone Else Where Both Of You Must Trust Each Other With Something Big And/Or Small):

Fill In At Night

The Result Of The Trust Transaction And How I Am Handling The Result: _____.

Date: _____   Mood: _____

Today I Am Taking A Leap Of Faith By:	I Believe:
What I Trust God To Do Today:	I Trust Myself To:
I Feel Free In Letting Go Of The Fear Of:	An Example Of Something That I Rely On Everyday That I Trust:
Something That Didn't Work Out For Me Yesterday That I Am Okay With:	It's Okay That I Cannot Control:
I Am Deciding That My Past Will No Longer Dictate:	Today's Pending Trust Transaction (Between You And Someone Else Where Both Of You Must Trust Each Other With Something Big And/Or Small):

Fill In At Night

The Result Of The Trust Transaction And How I Am Handling The Result: _____.

Date: Mood:

Today I Am Taking A Leap Of Faith By: | I Believe:

What I Trust God To Do Today: | I Trust Myself To:

I Feel Free In Letting Go Of The Fear Of: | An Example Of Something That I Rely On Everyday That I Trust:

Something That Didn't Work Out For Me Yesterday That I Am Okay With: | It's Okay That I Cannot Control:

I Am Deciding That My Past Will No Longer Dictate: | Today's Pending Trust Transaction (Between You And Someone Else Where Both Of You Must Trust Each Other With Something Big And/Or Small):

Fill In At Night

The Result Of The Trust Transaction And How I Am Handling The Result: _____.

My Trust & Truth Notes

Trust & Truth

Date: _____   Mood: _____

Today I Am Taking A Leap Of Faith By:	I Believe:
What I Trust God To Do Today:	I Trust Myself To:
I Feel Free In Letting Go Of The Fear Of:	An Example Of Something That I Rely On Everyday That I Trust:
Something That Didn't Work Out For Me Yesterday That I Am Okay With:	It's Okay That I Cannot Control:
I Am Deciding That My Past Will No Longer Dictate:	Today's Pending Trust Transaction (Between You And Someone Else Where Both Of You Must Trust Each Other With Something Big And/Or Small):

Fill In At Night

The Result Of The Trust Transaction And How I Am Handling The Result: _____.

I Will Not
Allow The Lie
That Someone
Told Me About
Myself To
Become
My Truth.

I Rely

On The

Truth.

I Have A Big And Loving Heart. I Am Always Willing To Give Love Another Chance. Love Is My Truth.

Made in the USA
Lexington, KY
09 December 2019